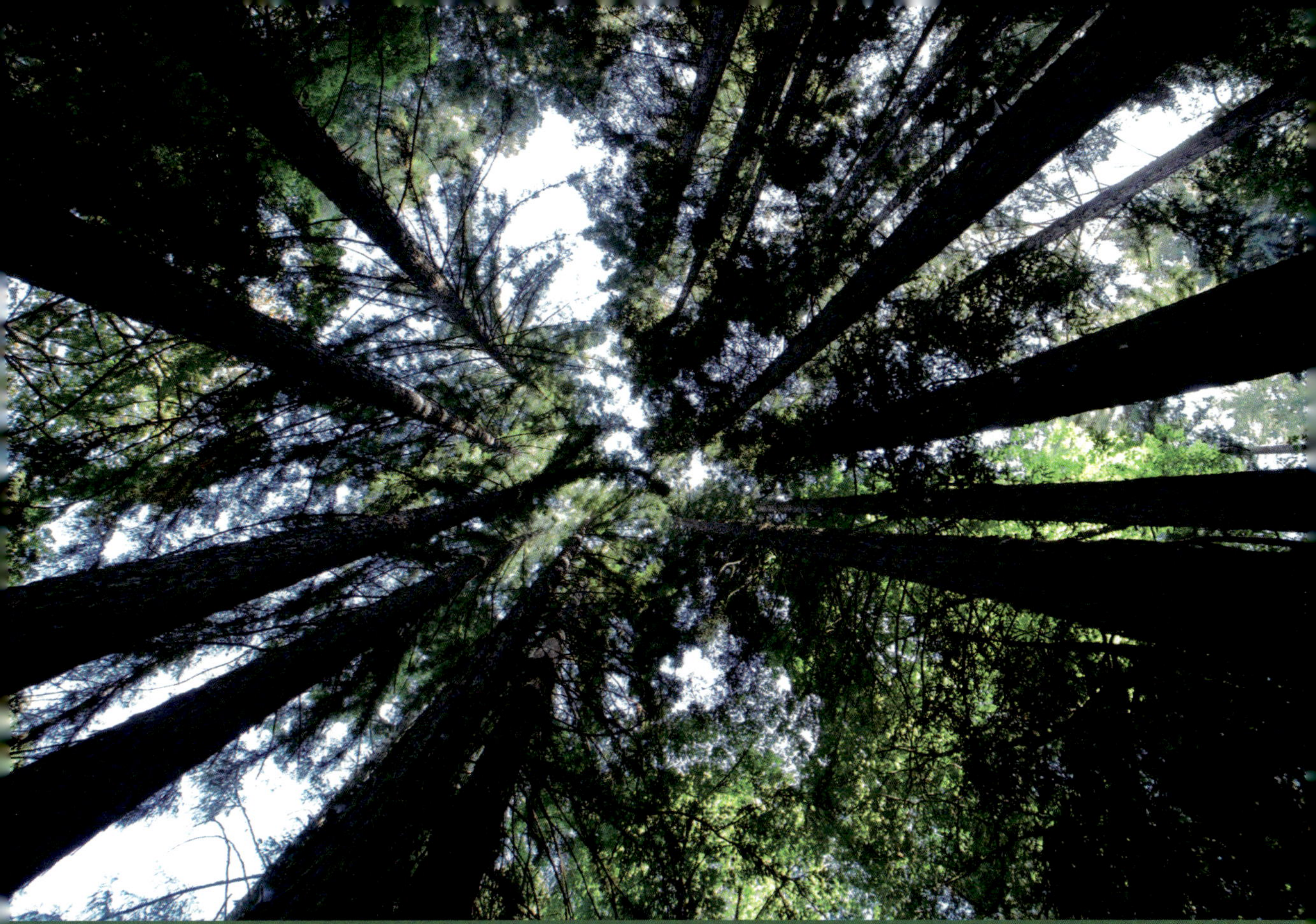

Natural Resources

FORESTS

Jason McClure and Piper Whelan

LIGHTBOX
openlightbox.com

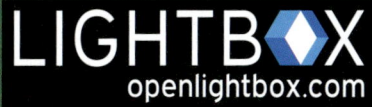

Go to
www.openlightbox.com
and enter this book's
unique code.

ACCESS CODE

LBU49696

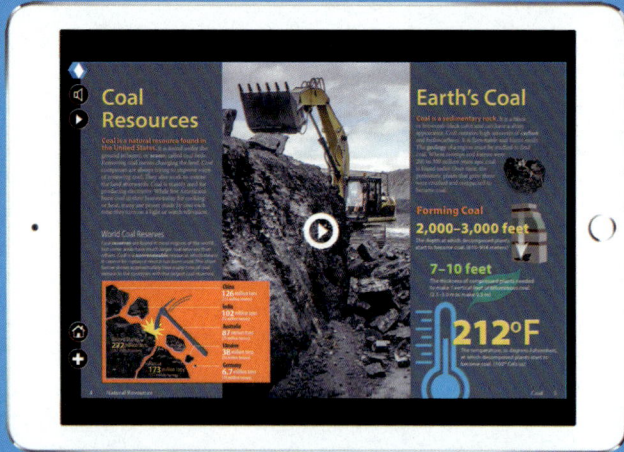

Lightbox is an all-inclusive digital solution for the teaching and learning of curriculum topics in an original, groundbreaking way. Lightbox is based on National Curriculum Standards.

STANDARD FEATURES OF LIGHTBOX

 AUDIO High-quality narration using text-to-speech system

 ACTIVITIES Printable PDFs that can be emailed and graded

SLIDESHOWS Pictorial overviews of key concepts

VIDEOS Embedded high-definition video clips

WEBLINKS Curated links to external, child-safe resources

 TRANSPARENCIES Step-by-step layering of maps, diagrams, charts, and timelines

 INTERACTIVE MAPS Interactive maps and aerial satellite imagery

 QUIZZES Ten multiple choice questions that are automatically graded and emailed for teacher assessment

 KEY WORDS Matching key concepts to their definitions

Copyright © 2017 Smartbook Media Inc. All rights reserved.

2   Natural Resources

CONTENTS

2   Lightbox Access Code
4   Forest Resources
5   Where Forests Grow
6   Forests in the United States
8   Forest Products
9   Wood as Paper
10 Building with Wood
12 Wood as Energy
13 The Forest Industry
14 Working with Wood
15 Exporting Wood
16 Conserving Forests
18 Managing Forests
20 Forestry Jobs
21 Quiz
22 Activity
23 Key Words/Index
24 Log on to www.openlightbox.com

Forest Resources

Forests are an important natural resource of the United States.
Forestry is a major economic activity for much of North America. In the United States, the timber industry is strong in the Pacific Northwest, the Gulf states, and the South Atlantic coastal plains.

Trees in forests provide wood for people to use. They also give off oxygen through **photosynthesis**. Some forests have millions of trees and are the size of a small country. Others are very small, with only a few hundred trees. There are many different kinds of forests, such as rainforests and jungles. Whatever the kind or size, forests are important to the world.

Forests Around the World
Forests are found on six of the seven continents. They cannot grow in extremely cold or dry areas.

Map Legend
- Forested land
- Land

4 Natural Resources

Where Forests Grow

Forests cover 31 percent of the world's land surface, or almost 10 billion acres (4 billion hectares). Different types of forests grow in different parts of the world, depending on the **climate** of the area. Some forests need more rainfall, and others need longer growing seasons. These factors affect where a forest can grow. There are some areas of the world where forests do not grow. The cold polar regions of the Arctic and Antarctica do not have any trees at all. Dry, hot desert areas may have a few small trees, but they do not have large forests. There are also very few trees on wide-open plains, or on high, cold mountains.

57%
Percentage of forests in the United States that are privately owned

430 million
Number of acres of private forest in the United States (174 million hectares)

2.5 million
Number of acres of private forest that are protected by the U.S. government (1 million hectares)

Forests 5

Forests in the United States

Almost 1.9 million square miles (4.9 million square kilometers) of forest cover the United States. Forests make up 33 percent of the country's landscapes. Dense forests grow across the Appalachian Mountains and the Rocky Mountains.

The California coast is lined with giant redwoods, the tallest trees on Earth. Redwoods can grow for up to 1,000 years.

The United States has 155 **national forests**. The U.S. Forest Service manages these protected areas. The largest is Tongass National Forest in Alaska, which covers 17 million acres (6.88 million hectares) of land.

Tongass National Forest, Alaska. Tongass National Forest was established in 1907 by President Theodore Roosevelt with the intention of preserving the wildlife there. Today, scientists estimate that about 1,700 brown bears live on Admiralty Island alone.

Natural Resources

MAP LEGEND
- **Boreal Forests** grow in areas with cold temperatures
- **Temperate Forests** grow in areas with moderate temperatures
- **Tropical Forests** grow year round and are usually found near the equator
- **Mixed Forests** include vegetation from two or three forest types
- Rocky Mountains
- Appalachian Mountains
- United States
- Other Countries
- Water

Shoshone National Forest, Wyoming. Created in 1891, Shoshone National Forest was the first national forest in the United States. With 2.4 million acres (970,000 hectares), the forest includes sagebrush flats, meadows, and three different mountain ranges.

Tuskegee National Forest, Alabama. At just 11,349 acres (4,593 hectares), Tuskegee National Forest in Alabama is the smallest U.S. national forest. The land was originally purchased to reclaim eroded farmland during the Great Depression of the 1930s.

Forests 7

The forest products industry generates $200 billion a year for the U.S. economy.

Forest Products

Forests provide the material for products that Americans use every day. Families eat at wooden tables and keep their books on wooden bookcases. Students sit at wooden desks and use wood pencils and rulers. Trees also grow fruit and nuts for people to eat. Maple syrup is made from tree sap, and cinnamon comes from tree bark.

Items Made from Wood

From telephone poles to snow sleds, people use a variety of wood products in their lives.

Chairs

Guitars

Colored Pencils

Ladders

Wood as Paper

Everyone uses paper. There are about 345 paper mills in the United States. Paper mills use wood to make paper products. Mills chop wood into small pieces, then soften it with water. The soft wood is then flattened into paper. Paper is used for books and newspapers. The United States consumes about 25 percent of the world's paper. More than two billion books, 350 million magazines, and 24 billion newspapers are published in the United States each year. On average, each American uses more than 700 pounds (317.5 kilograms) of paper products every year.

A 40-foot (12-meter) tree with a diameter of 6 to 8 inches (15 to 20 centimeters) makes approximately one ream, or 8,333 sheets, of paper.

Paper Use by Country

The United States ranks seventh in the world for paper use. The average American uses about five and a half 40-foot (12-meter) tall trees worth of paper each year. Belgium uses more paper than any other country in the world, while Azerbaijan uses the least. See how personal paper use in the United States compares to that of other countries around the world.

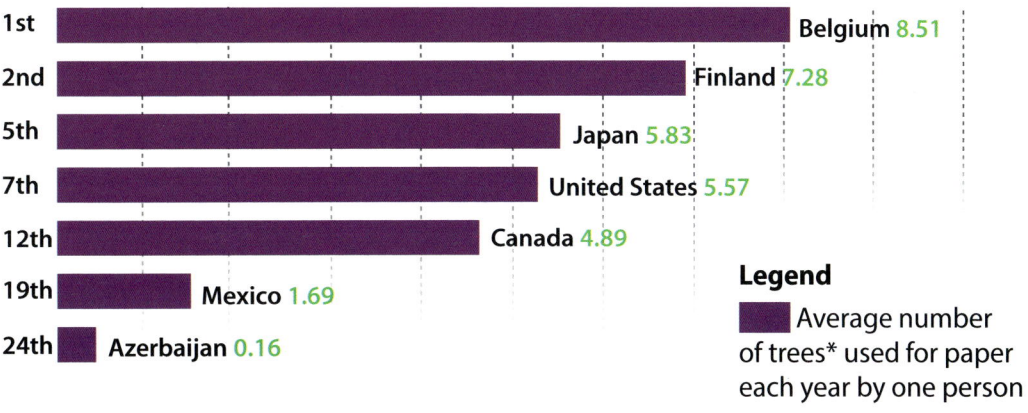

Rank	Country	Trees
1st	Belgium	8.51
2nd	Finland	7.28
5th	Japan	5.83
7th	United States	5.57
12th	Canada	4.89
19th	Mexico	1.69
24th	Azerbaijan	0.16

Legend: Average number of trees* used for paper each year by one person

*40-foot (12-meter) tall, 6 to 8 inches (15 to 20 cm) in diameter

Lumber is used to build the frame, or shape, of houses.

Building with Wood

Wood is used for building. The construction industry uses **softwood** lumber to make houses and other structures. Softwoods include pine, cedar, and spruce. The frame of a house uses more than 13,000 feet (3,962 meters) of lumber.

Furniture is made with **hardwoods** such as birch and maple. Softwood is also used in furniture. However, hardwood furniture is stronger and lasts longer than softwood. About 395,000 people work in the U.S. furniture industry.

Wood as Lumber

Finding Trees
The lumber process begins by finding the right trees. Loggers look for trees that are a good size. Often, the government must approve where the loggers can look for trees.

1

Cutting Down Trees
Once trees have been found, roads must be built to get to them. Trees are cut to clear paths for trucks and other large equipment. The selected trees are then cut down for lumber. Once cut down, the branches—and sometimes the bark—are removed.

2

Transporting Trees
Machines called loaders place the logs onto trucks. These loaders have large claws to pick up the logs. Logging trucks can carry many large logs at a time.

3

Processing Trees
Trucks deliver the logs to the sawmill. At the mill, the logs are unloaded and sorted by size and type of wood. Mill workers run the logs through large saws and machines that cut and shape them into boards of different sizes and lengths.

4

Selling Forest Products
Lumber is loaded onto trucks and delivered to stores. At the stores, people can buy the lumber they need. Lumber stores carry all kinds and sizes of wood for different types of projects, from building bird houses to picnic benches.

5

Forests

Wood as Energy

Not all wood is used to create products. Pulp and paper mills burn bark and other wood scraps to make heat and electricity for their businesses. Sometimes, they sell extra wood waste to other companies to use for energy. Wood is a **renewable resource**. Once it is used, it can be replaced. Using wood to make energy is better for the environment than using many other fuels. Being renewable makes wood a good source of energy for power companies. There are currently about 80 power plants in the United States that make energy from wood waste.

Approximately 11.5 million U.S. homes burn wood for heat.

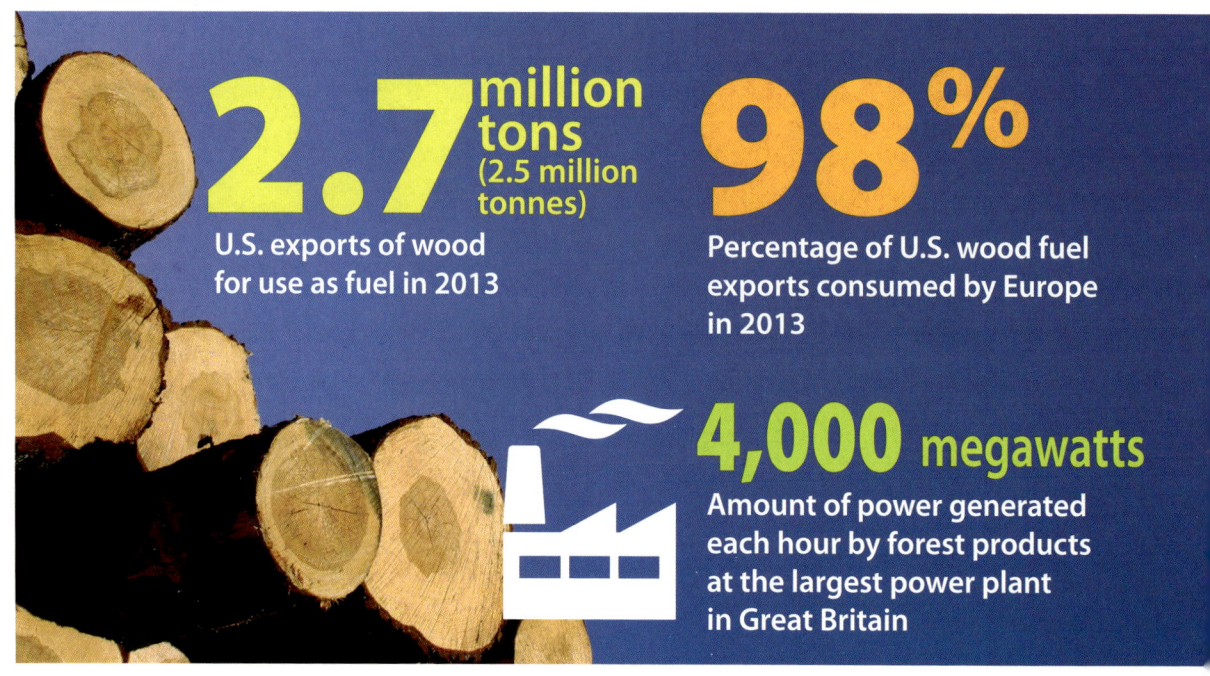

2.7 million tons (2.5 million tonnes)
U.S. exports of wood for use as fuel in 2013

98%
Percentage of U.S. wood fuel exports consumed by Europe in 2013

4,000 megawatts
Amount of power generated each hour by forest products at the largest power plant in Great Britain

12   Natural Resources

The Forest Industry

Each year, the United States produces about $17 trillion worth of goods and services. About $102 billion of that figure is generated by forest products, including pulp, paper, and other wood products. Goods and services include everything from electronics and entertainment to cars, furniture, and houses.

Six percent of all U.S. manufacturing dollars come from the forest industry.

Value of Forests to the U.S. Economy

Natural resources contributed 1.3 percent to the U.S. **gross domestic product** (GDP) in 2013. The forest industry is part of the natural resources sector of the United States. It contributed 0.1 percent of the money made in the United States in 2013.

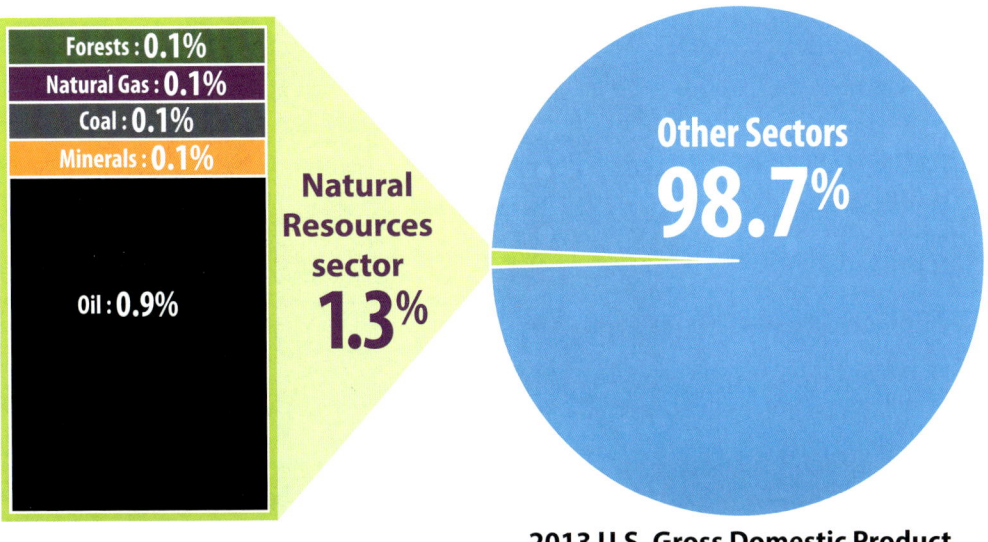
2013 U.S. Gross Domestic Product

Forests 13

The forest industry is one of the top ten manufacturing employers in the United States.

Working with Wood

The U.S. forest industry creates more than 926,000 jobs that work directly with trees and forests. Loggers cut down trees. Sawmill workers make trees into useful products. Other jobs use wood products to make other goods for sale. Construction workers build homes and buildings. Carpenters build furniture and other items from wood.

Forest Industry Jobs

Sawmill workers and loggers work with raw wood products. Most jobs in the forestry industry take those raw wood products and make new products from them. Paper and furniture are examples of products made from raw wood.

408,900
Wood Product Manufacturing Jobs

378,200
Pulp and Paper Manufacturing Jobs

139,000
Forestry and Logging Jobs

Exporting Wood

The United States makes a great deal of money from shipping forest products to other countries. In fact, the United States is fourth in the world for exporting wood products. China buys more U.S. wood products than any other country. In recent years China has bought more and more U.S. lumber. In 2014, the country bought more than $1 billion in U.S. hardwood lumber. Exporting wood pellets and chips for fuel has also recently become more profitable. In 2014, Great Britain bought 67 percent of U.S. wood pellet exports.

The United States exported $9.7 billion in forest products in 2014.

Where the United States Sends Wood

Most U.S. wood and wood products are sent to China. The second-largest buyer of U.S. wood products is Canada, followed by the European Union.

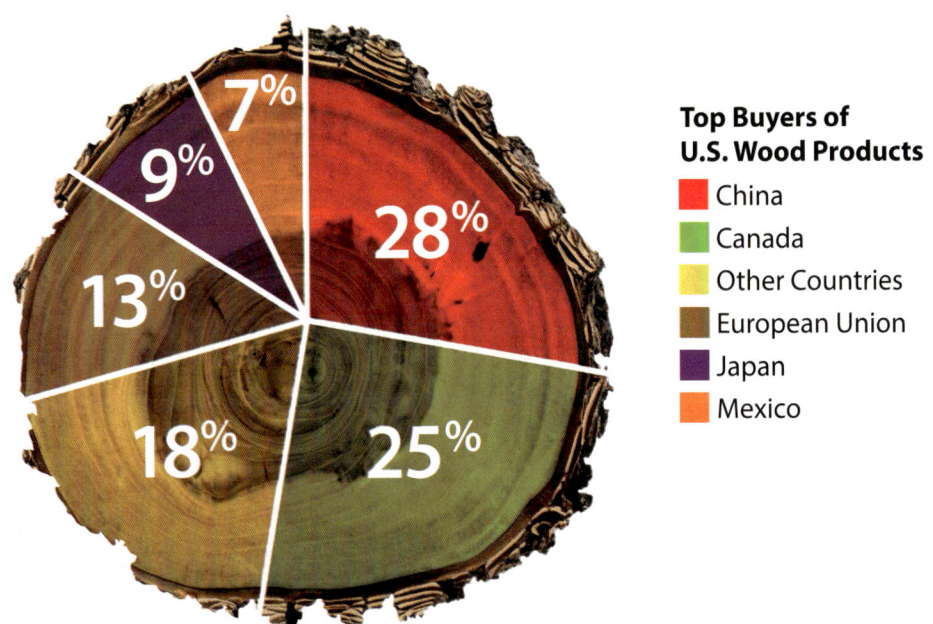

Top Buyers of U.S. Wood Products
- China
- Canada
- Other Countries
- European Union
- Japan
- Mexico

Forests 15

Conserving Forests

Forests are renewable resources. They can grow back and be used again, but this process may take decades. For this reason, logging companies must follow rules set by governments about cutting down trees. The United States has developed many different ways to manage forests. These include **sustainable forestry**, forest **certification**, and recycling.

In sustainable forestry, older, larger trees are removed because they provide the most wood. Some large trees are left to provide shelter for new trees to grow. When trees are removed, **saplings** are planted to replace them. With enough older trees left, the forest can repair the damage of tree removals.

A History of U.S. Forests

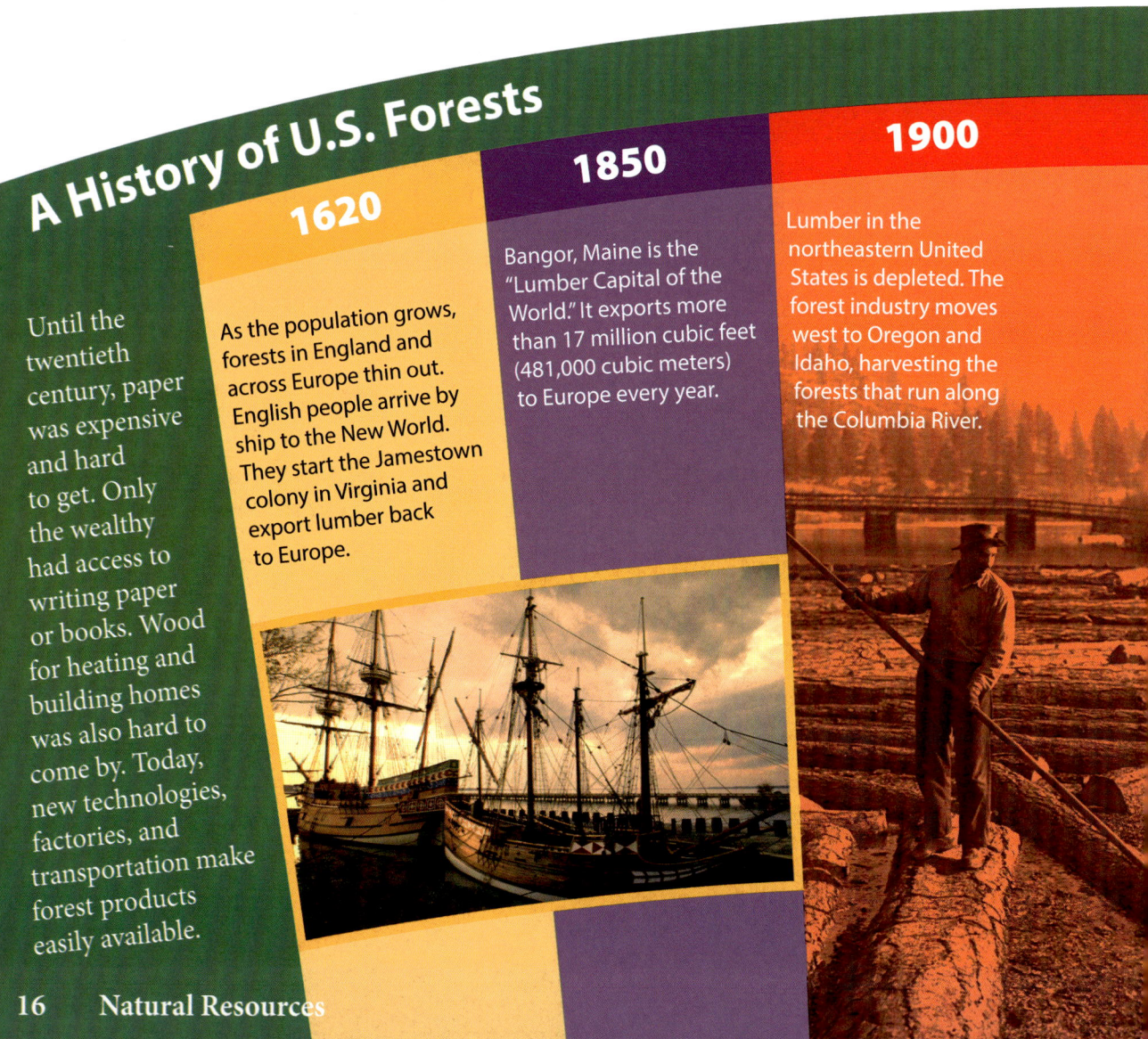

Until the twentieth century, paper was expensive and hard to get. Only the wealthy had access to writing paper or books. Wood for heating and building homes was also hard to come by. Today, new technologies, factories, and transportation make forest products easily available.

1620
As the population grows, forests in England and across Europe thin out. English people arrive by ship to the New World. They start the Jamestown colony in Virginia and export lumber back to Europe.

1850
Bangor, Maine is the "Lumber Capital of the World." It exports more than 17 million cubic feet (481,000 cubic meters) to Europe every year.

1900
Lumber in the northeastern United States is depleted. The forest industry moves west to Oregon and Idaho, harvesting the forests that run along the Columbia River.

If a logging company is practicing sustainable forestry, it can apply for forest certification. To be certified, a logging company has its logging practices checked. The logging company must be able to prove that it is only cutting down the trees it is allowed to by law and that it is not polluting the environment. Forest certification helps people know if the wood products they are buying came from a sustainable forest.

Fewer trees being cut down means fewer products made from newly cut wood. Recycling helps make up for this difference. Used paper is sorted by type, then softened with water. Materials such as paper clips and staples are removed. The paper is cleaned and any ink is washed away. Then, the clean paper is flattened and made into recycled paper. Using recycled paper products and forest certified products helps save trees.

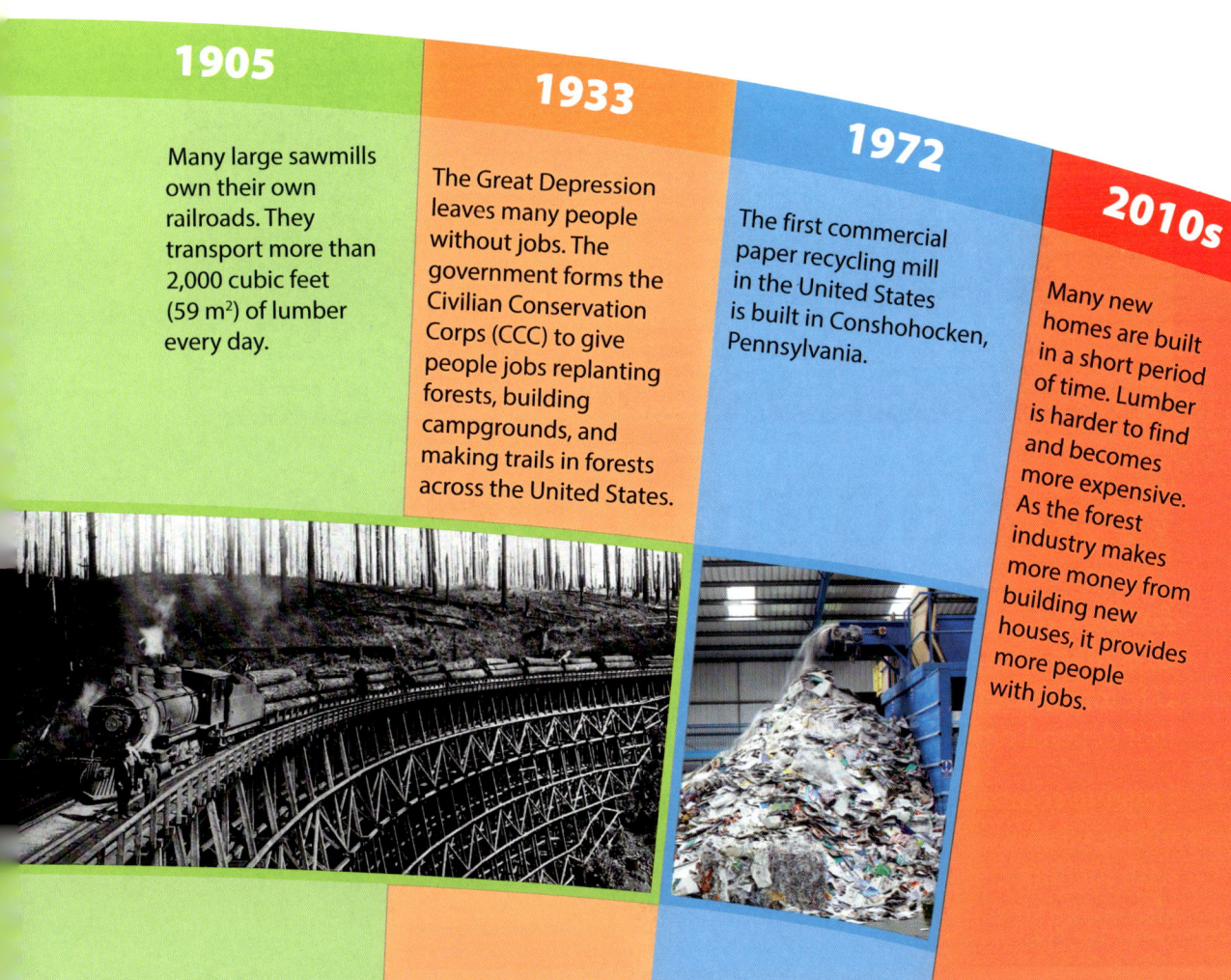

1905
Many large sawmills own their own railroads. They transport more than 2,000 cubic feet (59 m²) of lumber every day.

1933
The Great Depression leaves many people without jobs. The government forms the Civilian Conservation Corps (CCC) to give people jobs replanting forests, building campgrounds, and making trails in forests across the United States.

1972
The first commercial paper recycling mill in the United States is built in Conshohocken, Pennsylvania.

2010s
Many new homes are built in a short period of time. Lumber is harder to find and becomes more expensive. As the forest industry makes more money from building new houses, it provides more people with jobs.

Forests 17

About 106 million acres (43 million hectares) of public and private forests are protected by the U.S. government.

Managing Forests

As well as being an important resource for people, forests are also where many living things make their homes.
U.S. forests are home to thousands of species of plants and animals that depend on the forest to survive.

Logging companies must be careful about where they work and what kinds of trees they cut. Many individuals, groups, and government agencies work with logging companies to make sure that forests are used properly. They also make sure that the environment is affected as little as possible.

Governments
Governments set rules that guide how logging companies work. These rules tell loggers what kinds of trees they can cut down. Rules also limit the size of trees that can be cut and where loggers can work. Some forests are protected from logging by the government.

Individuals
Individuals play an important role in preserving American forests. Many people recycle paper materials and buy recycled items. This reduces the amount of trees that are cut down to make paper goods. People also work with environmental groups, governments, and logging companies to protect special forests. Old growth forests, for example, have trees that are hundreds of years old.

Companies
Logging companies work to make sure that forest resources are used responsibly. They hire tree planters to replace trees that have been cut down. Logging companies also look for better, less harmful ways to cut down trees.

Environmental Groups
Environmental groups work with governments and logging companies to make sure that trees are removed according to the rules. These groups also look for forests that need protecting. They bring this information to the government and logging companies. Some environmental groups also work with governments to make new laws to protect forests.

Forests 19

Forestry Jobs

The forest industry creates many kinds of jobs. Each job involves special tasks and training.

Logger

Duties: Cut down trees to be turned into lumber

Education: On-the-job training

Loggers are responsible for cutting down trees in forests. Cutting down trees can be dangerous. Loggers must watch for falling branches and be careful when handling the equipment. Loggers learn their job by training with other more experienced people.

Logging Pilot

Duties: Fly helicopters and remove large fallen trees

Education: Helicopter license and flying experience

Logging pilots fly helicopters to logging sites. The helicopters have large cables and hooks to pick up trees that have been cut. Pilots must have many years of experience flying before they can work as logging pilots.

Tree Planter

Duties: Plant saplings

Education: On-the-job training

Tree planters must go into an area that has been cleared of trees and plant new trees to take their place. One tree planter can plant more than 4,000 trees in a single day. Tree planters learn their job from more experienced workers.

Quiz

1. How much of Earth's land is covered in forests?
2. How many jobs does the forest industry support in the United States?
3. What are three ways the United States is managing its forests?
4. What kind of wood is usually used to build houses?
5. What percent of the landscapes in the United States are forests?
6. Which country buys the most U.S. wood products?
7. How many trees can a tree planter plant in a single day?
8. What is the value of the U.S. economy each year?
9. What was the nickname of Bangor, Maine, in 1850?
10. What did the CCC do?

ANSWERS
1 About 31 percent 2 About 926,000 3 Sustainable forestry, certification, and recycling 4 Softwood 5 33 percent 6 China 7 4,000 8 About $17 trillion 9 "Lumber Capital of the World" 10 Created jobs planting trees, building campgrounds, and making trails

Forests 21

Activity

How Do Forests Renew?

Materials Needed
notebook and pencil

Forests are made up of living things. When a tree dies, the wood starts to break down. Organisms eat parts of the wood, helping this process. Eventually, the dead tree becomes part of the soil. New trees use the nutrients in the soil to grow.

For this activity, you will need an adult to take you to a local forest. Take a notebook and pencil with you. Walk around the forest and look for a small fallen tree or log. Study the log. Turn it over. Is the log hard or soft? Can you break off small pieces of it? Can you see any organisms in the log?

Look for the ways the dead tree is helping to grow new trees. Write down your observations.

Key Words

certification: written or formal approval that certain standards or rules have been met

climate: the regular weather conditions in a certain area

gross domestic product: a measure of the value of all the goods and services produced in an economy in a given period of time

hardwoods: hard, compact woods that come from trees that have needles instead of leaves

national forests: forests that are owned and maintained by the U.S. federal government

photosynthesis: a plant process that turns carbon dioxide and water into oxygen and glucose

renewable resource: any natural resource that can be replaced

saplings: young trees

softwood: wood that is less dense and comes from trees that shed their leaves in winter

sustainable forestry: a responsible way of using and caring for forests that helps maintain their value over time

Index

boreal forests 7

forest industry 13, 14, 16, 17, 20, 21
furniture 10, 13, 14

loggers 11, 14, 19, 20
logging companies 16, 17, 18, 19
lumber 10, 11, 15, 16, 17, 20, 21

manufacturing 13, 14
mixed forests 7

paper mills 9, 12
pine 10
pulp 12, 13, 14

recycling 16, 17, 19, 21
redwoods 6
resources 4, 12, 13, 16, 18, 19

sawmill 11, 14, 17

temperate forests 7
tropical forests 7

Forests 23

LIGHTBOX

➕ SUPPLEMENTARY RESOURCES

Click on the plus icon ➕ found in the bottom left corner of each spread to open additional teacher resources.

- Download and print the book's quizzes and activities
- Access curriculum correlations
- Explore additional web applications that enhance the Lightbox experience

LIGHTBOX DIGITAL TITLES
Packed full of integrated media

VIDEOS
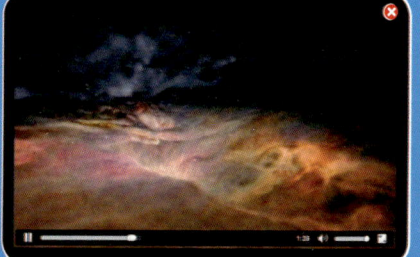

INTERACTIVE MAPS
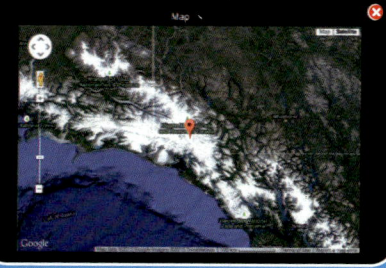

WEBLINKS

SLIDESHOWS

QUIZZES
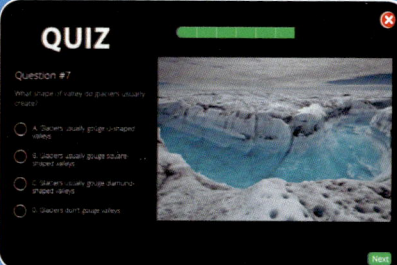

OPTIMIZED FOR
✓ **TABLETS**
✓ **WHITEBOARDS**
✓ **COMPUTERS**
✓ **AND MUCH MORE!**

Published by Smartbook Media Inc.
350 5th Avenue, 59th Floor New York, NY 10118
Website: www.openlightbox.com

Copyright © 2017 Smartbook Media Inc.
All rights reserved. No part of this publication may be reproduced, stored in a retrieval system, or transmitted in any form or by any means, electronic, mechanical, photocopying, recording, or otherwise, without the prior written permission of the publisher.

Library of Congress Control Number: 2016931222

ISBN 978-1-5105-1054-8 (hardcover)
ISBN 978-1-5105-1055-5 (multi-user eBook)

Printed in Brainerd, Minnesota, United States
1 2 3 4 5 6 7 8 9 0 20 19 18 17 16

052016
052016

Project Coordinator: Jared Siemens
Art Director: Terry Paulhus

Every reasonable effort has been made to trace ownership and to obtain permission to reprint copyright material. The publisher would be pleased to have any errors or omissions brought to its attention so that they may be corrected in subsequent printings.

The publisher acknowledges Getty Images, iStock, and Corbis Images as its primary image suppliers for this title.

24   Natural Resources